DATE DUE

JAN 2 3 '90			

The Library Store #47-0103

Mozart

Percy M. Young

Illustrations by Tony Morris

The Bookwright Press
New York · 1988

Great Lives

Beethoven
Louis Braille
Captain Cook
Marie Curie
Francis Drake
Einstein
Queen Elizabeth I
Queen Elizabeth II
Anne Frank
Gandhi
King Henry VIII
Helen Keller

Joan of Arc
John F. Kennedy
Martin Luther King, Jr.
John Lennon
Ferdinand Magellan
Karl Marx
Mozart
Napoleon
Florence Nightingale
Elvis Presley
William Shakespeare
Mother Teresa

First published in the
United States in 1988 by
The Bookwright Press
387 Park Avenue South
New York, NY 10016

First published in 1987 by
Wayland (Publishers) Limited
61 Western Road, Hove
East Sussex BN3 1JD, England

ISBN 0–531–18176–6

Library of Congress Catalog Card Number: 87–71471

Phototypeset by
Kalligraphics Ltd, Redhill, Surrey
Printed in Italy by G. Canale & C.S.p.A., Turin

92/
MOZ   c   1. Composers.
                    2. Mozart, Wolfgang Amadeus

Contents

A musical family in Austria   4
"Wonder children" at Court   6
Success in London   8
Honors in Italy   10
A difficult employer   12
The Emperor arranges a competition   14
The trials of a composer in love   16
"The greatest composer I know"   18
Master of comedy   20
The "Jupiter" symphony   22
A new look at old music   24
"The Magic Flute"   26
A mysterious stranger calls   28

Important dates   30
Glossary   31
Books to read   31
Index   32

A musical family in Austria

Every summer, music-lovers from all over the world flock to the Austrian city of Salzburg for its annual Mozart festival. This festival honors the city's most famous son, Wolfgang Amadeus Mozart, one of the greatest composers of all time.

Mozart was born in Salzburg on January 27, 1756. His parents already had a four-year-old daughter, Maria Anna, or "Nannerl" as she was nicknamed. But the coming of the son they had longed for was a special joy. Leopold and Anna Maria Mozart, who were devout Catholics, chose particular names for their only son. "Wolfgang" was the name of a saint who once had lived near Salzburg, and "Amadeus" meant dedication to God.

Leopold Mozart himself was a fine violinist, violin teacher and composer. He was one of many musicians in the service of the Archbishop of Salzburg, who were employed to provide music for receptions at the Archbishop's palace and in the houses of wealthy citizens, as well as for services in the cathedral and

Salzburg, the beautiful Austrian city where Mozart was born.

churches of the city. When his son was a year old, Leopold Mozart was promoted to be a Court Composer.

In those days a son was often taught by his father to follow him in his trade or profession. It was the great hope of his parents that Wolfgang, like his father, become a musician. It soon became clear that Wolfgang was to exceed his parents' greatest hopes. He was no more than four when his father realized that he had special gifts. He could play little pieces on the harpsichord, or on the new instrument then taking its place, called the pianoforte. Soon he made up little dances and his father proudly wrote them down. Nannerl too was exceptionally talented, so, when Wolfgang was six, Leopold decided that he would take the children to perform in the important cities of Munich and Vienna.

The Mozart family home was always filled with music.

"Wonder children" at Court

Before Leopold Mozart could leave Salzburg he needed his employer's permission. This was readily granted by the Archbishop, who was pleased that important people in other cities should learn what talented children lived in Salzburg. So, early in 1762, Wolfgang and Nannerl found themselves for three weeks in Munich, the capital city of Bavaria. They were excited to be asked to play their pieces before the Elector, the

Nannerl, age 11, and Wolfgang, age 7, performing at Court.

ruler of Bavaria. Leopold was delighted with their reception and at once began to plan a more ambitious expedition.

Vienna was the capital of Austria and the chief city of the Holy Roman Empire. The Empire, as it was generally called, was ruled by an Emperor and Empress whose Court in those days was notable for its rich musical tradition. Opera, ballet, and instrumental music of all kinds flourished, with employment for performers and composers from many countries. The Mozarts spent the last part of 1762 in Vienna. Nannerl and Wolfgang, admired by courtiers and professional musicians alike, were regarded as "wonder children." Wolfgang could play the most difficult of keyboard pieces presented to him, even if he had never seen the music before. He could pass all the tests that could be thought of. Everyone was astonished at the six-year-old's talent.

Leopold was well pleased. The Empress, Maria Theresa, spoiled the children and gave them presents. And the courtiers were kind. They were all very concerned when Wolfgang fell ill with scarlet fever, the first of many illnesses brought on through continual travel and demanding tasks.

At the end of December, Leopold took the children to the far-distant city of Pressburg so that they could play to some Hungarian noblemen. The journey there and back was terrible. The carriages were driven across rough, frozen roads. Leopold had a toothache, and, to make matters worse, he got back too late to perform his Christmas duties in Salzburg.

Wolfgang suffered from the strain of traveling and playing.

Success in London

Although Leopold Mozart was a fine violinist and an efficient composer, he was more than ready to act as his son's manager. For ten years, from the age of six to sixteen, Wolfgang was almost constantly on the move. He grew up to be a master performer on the piano and the organ, a good violinist, and a dazzling composer. Although Nannerl traveled with her father and brother, and was herself an

Johann Christian Bach, who helped Mozart during his visit to London.

accomplished, performer, it was Wolfgang who stole the limelight as they visited the courts that lay along the valley of the Rhine.

Europe was then a patchwork of many states. Some were big, some small; some were powerful, while many were not. The rulers and their courtiers were rich, but their servants and subjects were poor. Except for a favored few, the musicians employed at these courts were treated as servants. As he grew up, Wolfgang discovered this and it made him angry. Musicians, however, were

Mozart was an outstanding pianist as well as a brilliant composer.

generous to him, and at the famous court at Mannheim he was able to learn all about the kind of orchestral music developed there. It was there that he studied the form of the symphony and the newly introduced instruments, particularly the clarinet, which brought new sounds into musical composition.

Musicians then being "citizens of the world," the Mozarts were not surprised to find that the chief musician in London was a German. This was Johann Christian Bach, son of the famous Johann Sebastian Bach of Leipzig. Johann Christian was kind to Wolfgang and helped him to compose his earliest symphonies.

The Mozarts spent more than a year in England, where Wolfgang astonished people with his compositions and his performances on the piano and organ. The English loved choral music, and in gratitude for many kindnesses Wolfgang composed a motet, *God is our refuge*, of which the manuscript is still to be seen in the British Museum.

Despite his genius, Mozart was often treated like a servant.

Honors in Italy

Italy was the great land of song. Opera, which brings together drama and music, was invented in Italy. Even today we are reminded of the importance of Italian music in earlier times by the many Italian musical terms in general use, such as *allegro, andante, pizzicato* and many others.

Wolfgang had heard much Italian music and eagerly showed how well he understood its melodies, rhythms and harmonies. He seemed by instinct to know how to develop them and to give them shape. Most important, knowing the Italian language almost as well as his own, he could bring words to life. This he showed in his first *opera buffa* (comic opera), *La finta semplice* (Pretending to be stupid), performed before the Archbishop of Salzburg. At the same time Wolfgang was composing much sacred music, set to Latin words, and instrumental music of all kinds.

At the beginning of January 1770, just before his fourteenth birthday, Wolfgang and his father arrived in Italy for an extended stay. Wolfgang's fame had gone before him. In Verona the principal nobleman, Count Firmian, was interested in meeting the boy, for he had himself once been a violin pupil of Leopold's. Having heard from the German musician Johann Hasse how good Wolfgang's music was, Count Firmian invited him to compose an opera for performance in Milan.

This was an *opera seria* (serious opera), an opera about a hero of ancient times. In this case the hero was Mithridates (the title of the opera) who was an Asian prince who fought against the Romans. With this and other works Wolfgang won the praise of the learned musicians of Verona, Bologna and Milan, and of the Pope. When Mozart wrote down from memory the music of a motet that he had heard only once, the Pope awarded him the Order of the Golden Spur.

In Italy, the fourteen-year-old Mozart began to write operas. He wrote in Italian, which sounded lively and suited the music.

10

A difficult employer

Mozart was never very modest. After seeing as much of the world as he had so far, he came to two conclusions. One was that there was not a better composer anywhere than he was. The other, that he could not stay in Salzburg to be told what to do by an Archbishop who liked hunting better than music. This was the new Archbishop who came to rule

Mozart worked hard, producing compositions of many kinds.

Salzburg in 1772. Leopold waited until Wolfgang had written some music for occasions in the Archbishop's cathedral and castle and then took him back to Italy.

This visit, too, was a triumph. Wolfgang composed works that were brilliant even by Italian standards. Among them was another *opera seria*, called *Lucio Silla*. The hero was a Roman dictator who started as a bad character, but in the opera, at least, ended his career as reformed. Soon after this opera, Mozart composed one of the most exciting works for soprano voice and orchestra ever composed. This was the motet *Exsultate jubilate* (Rejoice and be glad).

By the time he was twenty-one Mozart had composed works of many different kinds. There were piano sonatas and concertos, in which he showed how smooth and expressive, and how brilliant and exciting, this new instrument was. There were symphonies, each with three or four contrasted sections. There was church music, for village churches as well as the great town churches. There were string quartets, which people compared favorably with those of the great

The cathedral in Salzburg, where Mozart was employed.

older master Josef Haydn.

Leopold hoped all the time that his son would obtain some well-paid post in a great city. But all that came was a minor job as Court organist in Salzburg. The day arrived, however, when the Archbishop thought that the young Mozart was too conceited and should be treated with contempt. When he was kicked downstairs in the Archbishop's palace, Mozart decided that he had had enough. One day in 1781, he walked out of the Archbishop's service to try his luck in Vienna. Delighted to be free, Mozart announced "Today is my lucky day."

The Emperor arranges a competition

Mozart was anxious to go to Vienna because the new Emperor, Joseph II, who was crowned in 1780, not only loved music but was also a good performer. He played the cello well enough to be able to take part in chamber music with the best of his court musicians. He helped to found music societies and concert organizations. But music in Vienna was not just for the well-to-do, for splendid concerts of the finest music took place in the beautiful public parks of the city.

Hardly had he settled into his new lodgings than Mozart was commanded to appear at court. The Emperor intended that Mozart should test his skills as pianist against those of the brilliant young Englishman (of Italian descent), Muzio Clementi. Both young men were inspired to give outstanding performances. The Empress decided that Mozart was the winner. Perhaps, she was a little biased, but the publicity was a help to Mozart.

He arranged concerts of his own, and was given opportunities to produce new works in public as well as private concerts. A former Salzburg mayor, Sigmund

Haffner, for whose daughter Mozart had once composed a cheerful Serenade, asked him to write a symphony for a family occasion. The "Haffner" symphony is one of Mozart's gayest works.

On July 16, 1782 the Opera House in Vienna was crowded to hear a new opera. The words were German – a welcome change from Italian! It was Mozart's *Die Entführung* (The Elopement) – all about helping damsels in distress. The opera was successful not only in Vienna but also in Prague and Warsaw. Because the story was set in Turkey, Mozart introduced Turkish sounds, made by the bass drum and cymbals.

Mozart and Clementi competing in front of the courtiers in Vienna.

The trials of a composer in love

When he had arrived in Vienna in 1781 Mozart had taken lodgings in a house belonging to the family of a young woman he had fallen in love with, called Aloysia Weber. Aloysia was a talented young soprano at the Mannheim Court, the music of which Mozart had so much admired. Her voice was high and brilliant. She was Mozart's ideal singer (he thought) and he began to write music to show off her beautiful voice.

Constanze Weber married Mozart when she was eighteen.

Wolfgang wrote home regularly to his family. When it became clear that he was carried away by Aloysia, Leopold became alarmed. But the young couple went different ways to further their careers. Aloysia found another young man.

Aloysia had a younger sister, Constanze, who was living with her mother when Wolfgang arrived as a lodger. Constanze was anxious to leave home, and (conveniently) Wolfgang fell in love with her, too. Just after he had written the "Haffner" symphony, they were married. He was twenty-six and Constanze was eighteen. In Salzburg Mozart's father was unhappy about the marriage, for neither Wolfgang nor Constanze had any money. His father reckoned that, in an expensive society, the young people would always be poor. And so it turned out. Wolfgang and Constanze suffered continual ill-health and poverty. Babies were born, and some died.

In the summer of 1783 Wolfgang and Constanze visited Salzburg. Wolfgang took with him a partly finished new work, a solemn Mass for soloists, choir and orchestra. This was a thanksgiving for marriage. While in his native city Wolfgang discovered that an old friend, Josef Haydn's brother Michael, was too ill to write some violin duets that had been ordered. At once Wolfgang agreed to take on the job for him.

Mozart fell in love with Aloysia, but later married her sister.

"The greatest composer I know"

Some of the orchestral players of Salzburg were among Mozart's closest friends and drinking companions. Ignaz Leutgeb was one of them. He was a rough-mannered man, but he played the horn better than anyone for miles around. It was convenient when he, too, came to live in Vienna. Mozart could never resist beautiful sounds, and the way in which he could make the best use of the horn encouraged players to improve their skills. The best known of Mozart's works written for Leutgeb to demonstrate the qualities of the horn were four concertos for horn and orchestra.

Mozart used the concerto form (like the symphony, in several sections) to display the qualities of other wind instruments. His

crowning achievements in concerto form, however, are for piano and orchestra – in all twenty-five works. Mozart's performances of his own piano concertos had much to do with the development of the instrument. He amazed audiences not only by his brilliance but even more by the depth of his feeling, by his contrasting effects of loud and soft.

When musicians played together for their own pleasure in those days, the favorite instrumental combination was two violins, viola, and cello. This combination was called a string quartet. The great master of music for string quartet was the much-loved Haydn. When Mozart, twenty-five years his junior, settled in Vienna, Haydn used to visit him to play quartets. One day in 1785 Mozart had completed three new quartets. Leopold Mozart (Wolfgang's father) was in the house when Haydn called. He took Leopold aside to say, "I tell you, before God, and as an honest man, that your son is the greatest composer I know."

Josef Haydn, himself a great composer, was deeply impressed by Mozart's music.

Master of comedy

People are sometimes sad, sometimes cheerful. In one way or another all art deals with these opposite areas of experience. So, on the one hand there is tragedy, on the other comedy. The very greatest artists produce masterpieces both of tragedy and comedy.

Before he settled in Vienna, Mozart had composed comic operas as well as some of a more serious nature. The chief poet of the Imperial Theater recognized Mozart's rare musical skills and

Mozart delighted audiences with his comic operas.

Prague, where Mozart had another great musical triumph.

in 1785 asked him to make an opera out of a well known story about a barber. An unusual "hero," the barber, Figaro, was the center of a comedy at the expense of the well-to-do.

Le Nozze di Figaro (The Marriage of Figaro) was first performed on May 1, 1786 in Vienna. The part of Figaro was played by an Irishman, Michael Kelly; that of Susanna, the heroine, by Nancy Storace from England. Together with Thomas Attwood, who came from London to take composition lessons with Mozart, these were close friends of the composer.

A pretty, new theater had recently been built in Prague –

the capital of Bohemia – and Mozart was invited to perform his new opera there. Bohemia at that time was ruled from Vienna by the Emperor. The Bohemians hated that and longed for independence. So *The Marriage of Figaro* – a story that spoke up for the underdog and was full of wonderful tunes – was received rapturously. "Nothing is played, sung, or whistled but Figaro," it was said. The tunes were played at balls, in the taverns, in the streets. To show his appreciation of his reception, Mozart composed a new symphony for the people of Prague. It is now known as the "Prague" symphony.

A modern production of the popular Marriage of Figaro.

The "Jupiter" symphony

In 1787 Mozart enjoyed more success in Prague with his next comic opera, *Don Giovanni* (Don Juan). As always, hard pressed for time, Mozart arrived in Prague with the opera still unfinished. By working all night he completed the overture in time for the first performance. The reception of the opera was as enthusiastic as for *Figaro*. This was noticed in Vienna, and Mozart was given the post of chamber musician at Court. His main task was to write dances for the Court balls.

In that year Mozart's father died. Next year his baby daughter died. He was deeply in debt and driven to borrow money from a Viennese merchant, who belonged to the same society of

Mozart worked into the night to finish his scores in time.

The clavier on which Mozart composed Don Giovanni.

Freemasons as Mozart.

It was at this time, in spite of his hardships, that Mozart composed three works of such beauty that they are regarded as the very peak of musical excellence. These works were symphonies. The perfection of the symphony was the great achievement of the eighteenth-century "classical" style. Mozart, Haydn and Ludwig van Beethoven – a young man from northern Germany who came to Mozart for lessons in 1787 – were to become the great classical masters.

Mozart wrote his three greatest symphonies in six weeks in the

Mozart, Haydn and Beethoven: masters of classical music.

summer of 1788. The first is a stately work in the key of E flat major. The second, in G minor, is of tragic character. The third, in C major, has always been regarded as of special quality. In classical mythology Jupiter was the chief of the gods. Mozart's C major symphony of 1788 has long been known as the "Jupiter."

A new look at old music

A nobleman in Vienna, Baron van Swieten, sometimes engaged Mozart to give concerts. In 1788 he asked Mozart to arrange and perform some of Handel's oratorios. At that time neither Handel nor his great contemporary, Johann Sebastian Bach, were fashionable. But van Swieten recognized their great merit in spite of their music's not sounding "modern." As well as earning money at a time of hardship, Mozart was pleased to study the music of a great composer of a bygone age, and arrange it according to the style of his own day.

Winter was turning to spring in the next year when Mozart was invited to Dresden, to perform at the Court of the Elector of Saxony. Here he was well received and well rewarded. Next he went north to Leipzig, the city made famous by Bach. In the church of St. Thomas – where Bach had once worked – Mozart heard one of Bach's motets. "Here," he said, "is something from which one may learn."

From Leipzig he went to

Potsdam, near Berlin, where the King of Prussia had his summer palace. This King was greatly impressed with Mozart's music and asked him to compose a set of quartets. These, the three "King of Prussia" quartets, were the last works of this kind by Mozart.

A great composer enriches his own music by continual study. As

clarinet player Anton Stadler, he composed in 1791 the Clarinet Concerto and the Clarinet Quintet.

Below *The King of Prussia asked Mozart to compose music for him.*

Above *A grand and elegant eighteenth-century ball.*

he approached his last years, Mozart showed how he had learned from Bach's techniques to deepen the meaning of his own music. He also showed an increasing sense of instrumental tone colors. For his friend, the

"The Magic Flute"

At the beginning of 1790 the Emperor Joseph II died and was succeeded by Leopold I. Leopold was crowned in Frankfurt, and Mozart hoped that if he performed his new piano concerto there at the time of the Coronation he might be given a better post at Court. But the new Emperor took no notice of the fine "Coronation" concerto. Nor did he appreciate the comic opera that Mozart had written on the orders of Joseph II. This opera was *Cosi Fan Tutte* (Women are like that).

Emanuel Schikaneder, popular actor and manager of one of the Vienna theaters, was looking for a new work that would attract good audiences. He also hoped to play a leading part himself. He found an oriental fairy tale – a mysterious, magical story – and translated it into German. He asked his friend Mozart if he could make out of this a new kind of opera. Mozart was excited by the challenge. Here was

In The Magic Flute, *Mozart experimented with a new form of opera.*

something that was both tragedy and comedy, which would allow him to use all the resources of instruments and voices available to him. So that he could work undisturbed Schikaneder gave Mozart a little summer house.

The hero, Tamino, has a magic flute; so the opera was called *Die Zauberflote* (The Magic Flute).

On September 30, 1791, Mozart directed the first performance, in which Schikaneder, playing on a set of "magic" bells, played the comic part of Papageno, a bird-catcher. A week later Mozart wrote to his wife, "I have just returned from the opera, which was as full as ever!" The audiences knew that here was a new form of opera, with ideas from Italian, German and Austrian music all brought together.

A modern production of The Magic Flute.

A mysterious stranger calls

One day in July 1791, Mozart was working in his summer house when a man called to see him. He would not say who he was, only that he came with a message. A nobleman had told him to ask Mozart to compose a Requiem Mass – a Mass for the Dead. He would pay the composer well. But the nobleman wished to pass the music off as his own.

Mozart being asked to write a Requiem Mass – his final work.

Mozart agreed to this odd request.

As if this was not enough, he was asked to write another opera for Prague. This he did in eighteen days. When Mozart was then appointed Music Director at St. Stephen's Cathedral in Vienna, it seemed that his luck was turning at last.

But, before he could finish the music for the Requiem Mass, he fell ill. For some years Mozart had had bouts of illness. Doctors, then as now, disagree about the illness he was suffering from. As he finally took to his bed in November, 1791, Mozart feared that he had been poisoned. Whatever the cause, Mozart knew he would never finish the Mass. "Did I not tell you that I was composing this Requiem for myself?" he is reported to have said on the day of his death.

Mozart's final bout of illness lasted less than a month. He died on December 5, 1791, age only thirty-five. The Requiem was completed, after his death, by one of his pupils.

After Mozart's death his fame spread. As music printing developed, copies of his works became available in many countries and his reputation soon became worldwide. Because he achieved so much in a short life, legends grew up about his genius. Novels, as well as biographies, were written about him, and in 1979 the mystery of his life and character became the subject of Peter Shaffer's famous play, *Amadeus*, which was later turned into a highly acclaimed film.

That was the beautiful name chosen by his parents in the hope that he might be divinely inspired. His music seems to tell us that he was.

This charming memorial to Mozart can be seen in Vienna.

Important dates

1756 (January 27) Wolfgang Amadeus Mozart born in Salzburg, Austria.

1762 He and his sister "Nannerl" perform before the Elector of Bavaria in Munich, and at the Imperial Court in Vienna.

1763 The Mozarts visit Mannheim. Wolfgang learns all about the orchestra and the symphonies composed there. In London he meets the son of J.S. Bach, plays before distinguished audiences, and composes a sacred chorus.

1770 He begins to master the two types of Italian opera – *opera buffa* (comic opera) and *opera seria* (serious opera).

1772 A new Archbishop comes to Salzburg. Wolfgang composes sonatas, concertos, symphonies, chamber music and sacred music. Much time spent in Italy where Mozart is very honored.

1777 Mozart visits Paris with his mother, who falls ill and dies during their visit.

1781 The Archbishop gives his orders, which Mozart refuses to obey. He leaves Salzburg and settles in Vienna, hoping for regular employment at Court.

1782 (July 6) A German opera, *The Elopement*, which is successful in Prague and Warsaw as well as Vienna. (August 4) He marries Constanze Weber against his father's wishes.

1783 He and Constanze visit Salzburg, and Wolfgang helps Michael Haydn out of a difficulty.

1785 He completes a set of string quartets, and Josef Haydn praises the young composer when he meets Leopold Mozart.

1786 Mozart's London friends take part in the first performance of *The Marriage of Figaro*. Triumph in Prague, and Mozart writes "Prague" symphony as a tribute to its generous people.

1787 Another comic opera. Mozart saddened by the deaths of his father and his daughter. He gives lessons to Beethoven.

1788 The year of the three great symphonies.

1789 A northern tour by way of Dresden to Leipzig. The King of Prussia is interested in Mozart's work and orders three string quartets.

1791 Mozart writes his clarinet concerto and quintet for his friend Anton Stadler. As he struggles to finish a composition commissioned by a "mysterious stranger," Mozart falls ill. (December 5) He dies, leaving his requiem, his last composition, unfinished.

Glossary

Chamber music   Music to be played in a small room (Italian, *camera*) by a few performers.

Concerto   Musical work usually in three sections (movements) for solo instrument and orchestra.

Elector   Ruler of a State entitled to help to elect the Emperor (see Holy Roman Empire).

Freemasons   A secret society to which in Mozart's day many artists and writers opposed to dictatorial government belonged.

Harpsichord   A keyboard instrument in which strings are plucked with quills; forerunner of the pianoforte (or, as we usually say, piano).

Holy Roman Empire   Empire in Central Europe from A.D. 800 to 1806.

Key   A group, or "scale," of related musical notes. The lowest note of the group gives its name to music based on that group: a sonata in C major.

Mass   The principal service of the Catholic Church, set to music appropriate to different occasions and festivals.

Motet   A work for voices, often without instruments, on a sacred text.

Pianoforte   The piano, successor to the harpsichord, with felted hammers and wire strings. So named because it could alternate between *piano* (Italian, "soft") and *forte* ("loud").

Quartet   A musical work for four instruments, usually in the form of a sonata.

Quintet   A musical work for five instruments.

Sonata   A work in three or four movements for solo instrument, or one instrument with keyboard accompaniment.

Soprano   A woman's high voice, useful for heroines in opera.

Symphony   Musical work for orchestra in three or, usually, four movements, developed during the eighteenth century.

Books to read

A Concise History of Music by Percy M. Young. D. White, 1973.

Enjoying the Arts by David Rattner. The Rosen Group, 1975.

Heroes and Heroines in Music by Wendy-Ann Ensor. Oxford University Press, 1981 (cassette also available).

Living Music by Keith Spence. Franklin Watts, 1979.

The Magic Flute and Other Children's Stories. China Books, 1981.

Mozart by Alan Kendall and Benjamin Britten. Silver Press.

Index

Amadeus 29
Attwood, Thomas 21

Bach, Johann
    Christian 8,
    9
Bach, Johann
    Sebastian 9, 24, 25
Bavaria, Elector of 6
Beethoven, Ludwig van
    23
Bologna 10

Clementi, Muzio 14
Cosi Fan Tutti 26

Don Giovanni 22
Dresden 24

Empire, the 6, 21

Firmian, Count 10

Haffner, Sigmund 14–
    15
"Haffner" Symphony 15
Handel, George
    Frederick 24
Hasse, Johann 10
Haydn, Josef 13, 19, 23
Haydn, Michael 17

Joseph II, Emperor 14, 26
"Jupiter" Symphony 23

Kelly, Michael 21

Leipzig 24
Leopold I, Emperor 26
Leutgeb, Ignaz 18
London 8–9

Magic Flute, The 26–7
Mannheim 8, 16
*Marriage of Figaro,
    The* 21, 22
Milan 10
Mozart, Anna Maria 4
Mozart, Constanze 16,
    27
Mozart, Leopold 4, 5, 6,
    7, 8, 10, 13, 16, 19, 22
Mozart, Maria Anna
    ("Nannerl") 4, 5, 6, 8
Mozart, Wolfgang
    Amadeus, born in
        Salzburg 4
    early travels 6–10
    decorated by the
        Pope 10
    leaves the
        Archbishop's service
        13
    a piano competition
        14
    a German opera 15
    in love 16
    as instrumentalist
        5, 8, 9 19
    a mysterious
        stranger 28–9
    death 29

chamber music 13,
    17, 19, 24
concertos 13, 18–19,
    25, 26
operas10, 13, 15, 20,
    21, 26–7
symphonies 9, 13 15,
    21,23
sacred music 9, 10,
    13, 17, 28–9
Munich 5, 6

Potsdam 24
Prague 15, 21, 22, 29
Pressburg 7
Prussia, King of 24

Requiem Mass 28–9

Salzburg 4, 6, 7, 12, 13
    16, 17, 18
Salzburg Archbishop of
    4, 6,12–13
Schikaneder; Emanuel
    26
Shaffer, Peter 29
Stadler, Anton 25
Storace, Nancy 21
Swieten, Baron van 24

Verona 10
Vienna 5, 13, 14–15,
    16, 18, 21, 22, 26, 29

Warsaw 15
Weber, Aloysia 16
Weber, Constanze *see*
    Mozart, Constanze

Picture credits

BBC Hulton Picture Library 6, 8 (below); Mary Evans Picture Library 8 (above), 10,
Camilla Jessel 27; John Topham Picture Library 13, 21 (above and below), 23 (below
ZEFA 4, 29. Cover artwork by Tony Morris.